Financial Mastery Blueprint:

Navigating Your Path to Prosperity

A Comprehensive Guide to Achieving Lasting Financial Freedom

MICHAEL LAMACCHIA

~DEDICATON~

DEDICATED TO MY MOTHER, LYNETTE, WHOSE UNWAVERING BELIEF IN ME HAS BEEN THE CORNERSTONE OF MY JOURNEY. YOUR ENDLESS SUPPORT AND ENCOURAGEMENT HAVE SHAPED THE PERSON I AM TODAY. THANK YOU FOR TEACHING ME THAT WITH DETERMINATION AND RESILIENCE, ANYTHING IS POSSIBLE. YOUR BOUNDLESS LOVE AND UNYIELDING SUPPORT HAVE BEEN MY GUIDING LIGHT. THE BELIEF YOU HAVE IN MY POTENTIAL HAS FUELED MY JOURNEY, AND I AM AND WILL BE FOREVER ETERNALLY GRATEFUL. I LOVE YOU BEYOND WORDS.

~CONTENTS~

Chapter 1: Financial Assessment

Embarking on the path to financial freedom requires a clear understanding of your current financial situation. This chapter serves as a foundational guide, supplying the tools necessary for a comprehensive financial assessment. By examining various sides of your financial landscape, you will be prepared to craft a robust plan for debt elimination and long-term financial well-being.

Income Evaluation:

Commence by dissecting all income sources. This includes your primary salary, bonuses, and any income from freelance work or side gigs. Distinguish between regular and irregular income streams for a holistic perspective.

Expense Breakdown:

Meticulously categorize your monthly expenses. Identify essential costs like housing, utilities, groceries, and entertainment. Draw a clear line between fixed and variable expenses to gain insight into your spending patterns.

Debt Inventory:

Compile a comprehensive list of outstanding debts—credit cards, loans, mortgages. Specify interest rates and minimum monthly payments. This inventory lays the foundation for prioritizing and strategizing debt repayment. -

Net Worth Calculation:

Calculate net worth by subtracting liabilities (debts) from assets (savings, investments, property). A positive net worth signifies financial health, while a negative net worth signals areas for improvement.

Emergency Fund Assessment:

Evaluate the sufficiency of your emergency fund. Aim for 3-6 months' worth of living expenses to create a crucial safety net for unexpected financial challenges.

Financial Goals Identification:

Define short-term and long-term financial goals. Whether saving for a home or education, articulate your goals and prioritize them based on urgency and significance.

Credit Score Analysis:

Check and understand your credit score, a pivotal factor influencing borrowing capabilities and interest rates. Understand the factors affecting your credit score for informed financial decision-making.

Insurance Review:

Assess your insurance coverage across health, home, and other assets. Ensure that your coverage aligns with your current needs and supplies adequate protection against potential financial risks. Regularly reviewing and updating your insurance policies is essential for staying prepared in the face of unexpected events.

Why Assess Insurance Coverage?

- Adequate insurance coverage safeguards against potential financial losses, offering protection and peace of mind. Regular reviews ensure alignment with current needs and mitigate risks associated with unforeseen events.

Explanation and Breakdown:

This chapter emphasizes the importance of thoroughly evaluating various aspects of personal finance. It begins with Income Evaluation, urging readers to dissect all income sources for a holistic view. The Expense Breakdown focuses on categorizing monthly expenses, differentiating between essential costs, and providing insights into spending patterns. The Debt Inventory guides readers in compiling a comprehensive list of outstanding debts, laying the foundation for a strategic repayment plan. Net Worth Calculation explains how to assess financial standing by subtracting liabilities from assets. Emergency Fund Assessment encourages readers to evaluate the sufficiency of their fund for unexpected challenges. Financial Goals Identification emphasizes setting short and long-term goals for a purposeful financial journey. Credit Score Analysis underscores the impact of credit scores on borrowing capabilities. The chapter concludes with an Insurance Review, highlighting the importance of regular assessments for preparedness in unforeseen events.

Key Takeaway:

Chapter 1 concludes with an emphasis on the critical importance of assessing insurance coverage. Understanding and addressing potential financial risks through insurance is a cornerstone of comprehensive financial planning. As you navigate the chapters ahead, may this foundation guide you toward a secure and informed financial future. Continue your journey in Chapter 2, where we explore the Psychology of Debt, unraveling the emotional and behavioral aspects that shape our financial decisions.

Chapter 2: Psychology of debt

Understanding the intricacies of debt goes beyond numbers; it delves into the psychological aspects that influence our financial decisions. This chapter explores the emotional and behavioral dimensions of debt, providing insights into how our mindset shapes our approach to borrowing and repayment.

The Emotional Impact of Debt:

Examine the emotional toll that debt can take, from stress and anxiety to feelings of guilt and shame. Understanding these emotions is the first step in developing a healthy relationship with debt.

Identifying Triggers for Debt Accumulation:

Explore common triggers that lead to accumulating debt, such as impulsive spending, lifestyle inflation, or unexpected emergencies. Recognizing these triggers empowers individuals to address root causes.

Overcoming the Stigma of Debt:

Discuss social beliefs surrounding debt and challenge any stigmas associated with it. Recognize that debt, when managed responsibly, can be a tool for achieving financial goals.

Mindfulness in Financial Decision-Making:

Introduce mindfulness techniques to enhance awareness of financial choices. Mindful decision-making reduces impulsive behavior and fosters intentional financial actions.

Coping Mechanisms for Financial Stress:

Provide coping mechanisms for dealing with financial stress. This includes creating a support system, practicing self-care, and seeking professional help when needed.

Breaking the Cycle of Debt:

Explore strategies for breaking the cycle of debt, including creating a realistic budget, negotiating with creditors, and seeking financial education. Breaking the cycle requires initiative-taking steps toward financial wellness.

Shifting from a Consumer to a Saver Mindset:

Encourage a shift from a consumer mindset focused on instant gratification to a saver mindset emphasizing long-term financial goals. This shift is crucial for sustainable debt management.

Celebrating Financial Wins:

Emphasize the importance of celebrating financial successes, no matter how small. Recognizing achievements boosts confidence and motivates continued progress.

Explanation and Breakdown:

Understanding the emotional impact of debt is crucial for comprehensive debt management. Finding triggers allows informed decisions, overcoming societal stigmas fosters a healthy mindset, and mindfulness reduces impulsive choices. Coping mechanisms ensure mental well-being, strategies break the debt cycle for stability, and shifting to a saver mindset is foundational. Celebrating financial wins reinforces positive behavior.

Key Takeaway:

Chapter 2 delves into the psychology of debt, shedding light on the emotional and behavioral aspects that influence financial decisions. By exploring triggers, coping mechanisms, and mindful decision-making, individuals can develop a healthier relationship with debt and pave the way for a more resilient and positive financial future.

Chapter 3: Strategies for Effective Budgeting

Effective budgeting serves as the cornerstone of financial stability. In this chapter, we will explore practical strategies to create and maintain a budget that aligns with your financial goals.

Establishing a Realistic Budget:

Creating a budget is an art and a science. Begin by crafting a budget that reflects your income, expenses, and financial objectives. Setting achievable spending limits in each category ensures that your budget becomes a realistic tool for financial equilibrium.

Tracking and Monitoring Expenses:

Regularly tracking and monitoring your spending is essential for financial awareness. Discover tools and apps that simplify the process, providing real-time insights into your financial habits. This awareness is the key to making informed decisions and avoiding unnecessary debt.

Adjusting the Budget as Needed:

Recognize the dynamic nature of life and finances. Learn how to adjust your budget to accommodate unexpected expenses or shifts in income. This adaptability ensures that your budget remains a relevant and practical guide on your financial journey.

Prioritizing Savings in the Budget:

Savings should be at the forefront of your financial plan. Uncover the significance of prioritizing savings within your budget. Explore strategies to allocate funds for emergency savings, retirement, and other long-term financial goals. Prioritizing savings is a crucial step towards building financial security.

Identifying and Eliminating Budget Leaks:

Budget leaks can silently drain your finances. Pinpoint communal areas where you might be overspending and develop skills to eliminate unnecessary expenses. By identifying and plugging these leaks, you optimize your budget for maximum efficiency.

Explanation and Breakdown:

Budgeting is not just about numbers; it is a dynamic tool that adapts to your life. Establishing a realistic budget, tracking expenses, and prioritizing savings are vital steps.

Key Takeaway:

Chapter 3 offers actionable insights into effective budgeting, emphasizing adaptability and strategic planning. As you implement these strategies, may your budget become a powerful ally in achieving your financial aspirations.

Chapter 4: Conquering Debt for Financial Freedom

Conquering debt is a pivotal step toward achieving financial freedom. This chapter explores proven strategies to navigate and triumph over your debts, paving the way for a more secure and empowered financial future.

The High-Interest Debt Battle:

High-interest debt can be a formidable opponent. Understand its impact on your financial health and learn why prioritizing and aggressively paying down high-interest debts is a strategic move. Conquering high-interest debt not only saves you money but accelerates your journey to debt freedom.

Strategic Choices: Snowball vs. Avalanche Method:

Two popular debt repayment methods, the debt snowball and debt avalanche, offer strategic choices. Delve into the strengths and weaknesses of each method and choose the one that aligns with your personality and financial goals. These methods provide structured approaches to tackle your debts systema.

The Art of Negotiation with Creditors:

Acquiring negotiation skills can make a momentous change in your debt repayment journey. Engage with creditors to explore options for reduced interest rates or extended payment terms. Effective negotiation can ease the burden of debt repayment, providing much-needed relief during challenging financial periods.

Crafting Your Personal Debt Repayment Plan:

Every financial journey is unique, requiring a personalized approach to debt repayment. Develop a plan tailored to your financial situation, understanding the importance of setting realistic milestones. Celebrate achievements along the way, turning your debt repayment plan into a roadmap for financial success.

Discipline to Avoid New Debt Accumulation:

While repaying existing debts is crucial, cultivating discipline to avoid accumulating new debt is equally important. Learn strategies to resist the temptation of adding to your debt load. Establish habits that promote financial discipline and responsible credit use.

Explanation and Breakdown:

Conquering debt requires a strategic approach, from prioritizing high-interest debt to crafting a personalized repayment plan. Negotiating with creditors and avoiding new debt accumulation further strengthens your path to financial freedom.

Key Takeaway:

Chapter 4 equips you with strategies for effective debt repayment, offering practical guidance to conquer debt and build a foundation for lasting financial stability. As you navigate these strategies, may each step bring you closer to a debt-free and empowered future.

Chapter 5: Building a Solid Credit Foundation

A solid credit foundation is crucial for financial health and flexibility. In this chapter, we will explore the intricacies of credit, understand how it impacts your financial life, and discuss strategies for maintaining a strong credit profile.

Understanding Credit Scores:

Demystify the world of credit scores. Learn how they are calculated, what factors influence them, and why they matter in various financial transactions. Understanding your credit score is the first step toward managing it effectively.

Maintaining a Positive Credit History:

Explore the significance of a positive credit history. Understand the impact of timely payments, credit utilization, and the length of your credit history. Maintaining a positive credit history opens doors to favorable interest rates and financial opportunities.

Responsible Credit Card Usage

Credit cards can be powerful financial tools when used responsibly. Learn strategies for responsible credit card usage, including paying balances in full, avoiding minimum payments, and managing credit limits wisely.

. Managing Existing Debts:

Managing your debts effectively is intricately connected to sustaining a robust credit base. Explore techniques for managing existing debts, understanding how they impact your credit, and strategies for minimizing negative effects.

Regularly Monitoring Your Credit:

Develop the habit of regularly monitoring your credit reports. Understand how to check for errors, unauthorized accounts, or suspicious activities. Initiative-taking credit monitoring is an initiative-taking step toward protecting your credit health.

Explanation and Breakdown:

Understanding and managing credit is a foundational aspect of financial literacy. From comprehending credit scores to responsible credit card usage, each element contributes to building a solid credit foundation.

Key Takeaway:

Chapter 5 equips you with the knowledge and strategies to build and maintain a solid credit foundation. As you implement these practices, may your credit become an asset, opening doors to financial opportunities and stability.

Chapter 6: Navigating Investments for Financial Prosperity

Investing is a key element in building wealth over time. This chapter aims to demystify investment basics, providing you with the knowledge and tools to make informed decisions that align with your financial goals.

Understanding Investment Vehicles:

Embark on a journey through the landscape of investment options, from traditional stocks and bonds to diversified mutual funds and real estate. Gain insights into the risks and rewards associated with different investment vehicles, empowering you to make informed choices tailored to your financial aspirations.

Setting Investment Goals:

Define your investment goals based on your unique financial aspirations and timeline. Whether it is saving for a dream home, funding education, or preparing for retirement, setting clear goals provides direction for your investment strategy and keeps you focused on long-term success.

Risk Tolerance and Diversification:

Assess your risk tolerance and embrace the concept of diversification. Learn how a diversified investment portfolio can mitigate risks and enhance the potential for returns. Tailoring your investments to your risk profile is key to weathering market fluctuations and achieving sustained growth.

Creating a Budget for Investments:

Allocate funds for investments within your budget. Understand the importance of consistent contributions to your investment accounts, fostering a disciplined approach that contributes to future financial growth and prosperity.

Long-Term vs. Short-Term Investments:

Distinguish between long-term and short-term investments, understanding the benefits and considerations for each approach. Align your investment choices with your financial goals and time horizon, creating a balanced and strategic investment portfolio.

Explanation and Breakdown:

Investing can be both exciting and daunting, and this chapter breaks down the fundamentals, from understanding various investment vehicles to setting goals, managing risk, and incorporating investments into your budget.

Key Takeaway:

Chapter 6 empowers you to embark on your investment journey with confidence. By understanding the fundamentals and aligning investments with your goals, you pave the way for future financial growth and security. As you navigate this financial landscape, may each investment decision bring you closer to your dreams and prosperity.

Chapter 7: Mastering Credit for Financial Empowerment

A robust credit foundation is essential for financial health and flexibility. This chapter delves into the intricacies of credit, illuminating its impact on your financial life and offering strategies for maintaining a strong credit profile.

Decoding Credit Scores:

Demystify the world of credit scores. Learn how these scores are calculated, the factors influencing them, and why they matter in various financial transactions. Understanding your credit score is the first step toward managing it effectively.

Nurturing a Positive Credit History:

Explore the significance of a positive credit history. Understand the impact of timely payments, credit utilization, and the length of your credit history. Maintaining a positive credit history opens doors to favorable interest rates and financial opportunities.

Navigating Responsible Credit Card Usage:

Credit cards can be powerful financial tools when used responsibly. Learn strategies for responsible credit card usage, including paying balances in full, avoiding minimum payments, and managing credit limits wisely.

Managing Existing Debts:

Effective debt management is intertwined with maintaining a strong credit foundation. Explore techniques for managing existing debts, understanding how they impact your credit, and strategies for minimizing negative effects.

Regularly Monitoring Your Credit:

Develop the habit of regularly monitoring your credit reports. Understand how to check for errors, unauthorized accounts, or suspicious activities. Proactive credit monitoring is a key step toward protecting your credit health.

Explanation and Breakdown:

Understanding and managing credit is a foundational aspect

of financial literacy. From comprehending credit scores to responsible credit card usage, each element contributes to building a solid credit foundation.

Key Takeaway:

Chapter 7 equips you with the knowledge and strategies to build and maintain a solid credit foundation. As you implement these practices, may your credit become an asset, opening doors to financial opportunities and stability.

Chapter 8: Sustaining Financial Wellness Through Insurance

Insurance is a cornerstone of financial stability, offering protection against unforeseen events. This chapter delves into the crucial role of insurance in sustaining financial wellness, providing insights into coverage types and strategies for comprehensive risk management.

Assessing Insurance Coverage:

Evaluate your insurance coverage for health, home, and other assets. Ensure that the policies in place provide adequate protection against potential financial losses. A thorough assessment lays the foundation for building a resilient financial safety net.

Mitigating Risks with Adequate Coverage:

Explore strategies to mitigate various financial risks through insurance. From health emergencies to property damage, having the right coverage ensures that unexpected events do not derail your financial stability. Discover the peace of mind that comes from knowing you are well-protected.

Understanding Policy Terms and Conditions:

Navigate the intricacies of insurance policies by understanding their terms and conditions. Familiarize yourself with deductibles, coverage limits, and exclusions. Clarity on policy details is key to making informed decisions and avoiding surprises during a claim.

Balancing Premium Costs and Coverage:

Strike a balance between premium costs and coverage. Understand how your insurance premiums impact your budget and explore ways to optimize coverage without compromising financial stability. This thoughtful approach ensures you get the protection you need without unnecessary financial strain.

Reassessing Insurance Needs Over Time:

Life changes, and so do your insurance needs. Regularly reassess your coverage as your circumstances evolve. Whether it is a new home, a growing family, or changes in health, adapting your insurance to align with your current situation is vital for sustained financial wellness.

Explanation and Breakdown:

Insurance is an initiative-taking financial strategy, and this chapter highlights the importance of assessing coverage, understanding policy details, and adapting to changing needs.

Key Takeaway:

Chapter 8 equips you with insights into sustaining financial wellness through insurance. As you navigate the world of insurance, may your coverage be a robust shield, protecting your financial stability in the face of life's uncertainties.

Chapter 9: Tax Strategies for Financial Optimization

Understanding and strategically navigating the realm of taxes is paramount for financial optimization. This chapter explores effective tax strategies that can enhance your financial well-being, providing insights into deductions, credits, and long-term planning.

Maximizing Deductions:

Delve into the world of tax deductions, uncovering opportunities to minimize taxable income. From business expenses to education costs, understanding eligible deductions ensures you keep more of your hard-earned money. Learn how to leverage deductions for maximum financial benefit.

Harnessing Tax Credits:

Explore tax credits as powerful tools for reducing your tax liability. Whether it is education credits, child tax credits, or energy-efficient home improvements, understanding and harnessing tax credits can lead to significant savings. Strategically utilize credits to optimize your financial position.

Long-Term Tax Planning:

Embrace an initiative-taking approach to long-term tax planning. Understand how decisions today can impact your tax situation in the future. From retirement contributions to investment strategies, align your financial decisions with a view toward optimizing your tax position over time.

Retirement Savings and Tax Efficiency:

Navigate the intersection of retirement savings and tax efficiency. Explore the tax advantages of various retirement accounts, from 401(k)s to IRAs. Learn how strategic contributions and withdrawals can maximize your retirement savings while minimizing your tax burden.

Seeking Professional Guidance:

Recognize the value of seeking professional guidance for complex tax matters. A qualified tax professional can provide personalized advice, ensuring you capitalize on available opportunities and adhere to ever-evolving tax laws.

Explanation and Breakdown:

Tax strategies are integral to financial optimization, and this chapter covers maximizing deductions, harnessing tax credits, long-term planning, and tax-efficient retirement savings..

Key Takeaway:

Chapter 9 equips you with essential tax strategies for financial optimization. As you incorporate these strategies into your financial plan, may your approach to taxes become a proactive and strategic element in your journey toward long-term financial well-being.

Chapter 10: The Path to Financial Freedom

The culmination of your financial journey leads to the threshold of financial freedom. This chapter explores the principles and practices that pave the way for true autonomy, providing a roadmap for achieving lasting financial freedom.

. Debt-Free Living:

Embrace the liberating power of debt-free living. Explore strategies to systematically eliminate debt, from high-interest obligations to mortgage payments. Debt freedom is a cornerstone of financial autonomy, providing flexibility and peace of mind.

Building Wealth and Investments:

Continue to build wealth through strategic investments. Explore diverse investment opportunities that align with your financial goals. Whether t is a diversified portfolio, real estate, or entrepreneurial ventures, strategic wealth-building opens doors to financial freedom.

. Sustainable Budgeting:

Transition from budgeting as a necessity to budgeting as a tool for sustainable financial wellness. Refine your budget to reflect your evolving needs and aspirations. A sustainable budget ensures continued financial stability and empowerment.

. Continued Learning and Adaptation:

Cultivate a mindset of continued learning and adaptation. Stay informed about financial trends, investment opportunities, and evolving tax strategies. A commitment to ongoing education positions you to make informed decisions for sustained financial success.

Giving Back and Philanthropy:

Explore the transformative power of giving back. As you achieve financial freedom, consider ways to contribute to causes you are enthusiastic about. Philanthropy becomes a fulfilling aspect of financial freedom, creating a positive impact beyond personal financial success.

Explanation and Breakdown:

Chapter Ten is the culmination of your financial journey, providing principles for lasting financial freedom. It emphasizes Debt-Free Living, encouraging strategies to eliminate various debts and gain flexibility. Building Wealth and Investments are discussed, suggesting diverse opportunities aligned with financial goals. Examining sustainable budgeting ii a sound strategy for continual financial well-being. The importance of Continued

Learning and Adaptation is highlighted, ensuring informed decisions for sustained success. Giving Back and Philanthropy are encouraged, transforming financial freedom into a means for positive impact.

Key Takeaway:

Chapter 10 marks the culmination of your financial journey. As you implement the principles outlined in this chapter, may you experience the profound liberation and empowerment that true financial freedom brings. May your path be one of enduring prosperity and positive impact.

Conclusion: Your Journey to Financial Mastery

Congratulations on completing the comprehensive journey through the chapters of this guide. As you reflect on the insights gained and strategies explored, remember that financial mastery is an ongoing journey rather than a destination. The principles and practices shared in this guide empower you with the knowledge and tools necessary for a lifetime of financial well-being.

Embracing Lifelong Financial Learning:

Financial literacy s a dynamic field, and staying informed is crucial. Cultivate a mindset of continuous learning, adapt to changes in the financial landscape, and explore new opportunities for growth. The commitment to ongoing education ensures you are well-equipped to make informed decisions that align with your evolving financial goals.

Building Resilience through Strategic Planning:

Financial resilience is born out of strategic planning. From debt elimination to wealth-building investments, each step contributes to your financial fortitude. A well-crafted budget, smart investments, and proactive risk management form the pillars of resilience, allowing you to navigate life's uncertainties with confidence.

Crafting Your Unique Path to Financial Freedom:

Financial freedom is not a one-size-fits-all concept. It is about crafting a path that aligns with your values, aspirations, and lifestyle. Whether it is achieving debt-free living, strategic wealth-building, or contributing to causes you care about, your journey to financial freedom is uniquely yours.

Empowering Your Future:

Financial empowerment is not just about accumulating wealth; it is about living a life aligned with your priorities. As you implement the principles shared in this guide, you may experience the empowerment that comes from making informed financial decisions, having control over your resources, and contributing positively to your community.

Your Continued Success:

Your success in mastering your finances is an ongoing process. As you move forward, remember that setbacks may occur, but each challenge presents an opportunity for growth. Stay resilient, adapt to changes, and celebrate the milestones on your journey. Your commitment to financial well-being is a powerful investment in your future.

45

Thank you for entrusting this guide with your financial education. May your path be one of sustained prosperity, fulfillment, and the lasting impact that comes from financial mastery.